THE DOMESTIC LIFE

1992 Agnes Lynch Starrett Poetry Prize

THE DOMESTIC LIFE

HUNT HAWKINS

University of Pittsburgh Press
Pittsburgh • London

The publication of this book is supported by a grant from the Pennsylvania Council on the Arts.

Published by the University of Pittsburgh Press, Pittsburgh, Pa. 15260
Copyright © 1994, Hunt Hawkins
All rights reserved
Manufactured in the United States of America
Printed on acid-free paper

Library of Congress Cataloging-in-Publication Data

Hawkins, Hunt.
    The domestic life / Hunt Hawkins.
        p.   cm. —(Pitt Poetry Series)
      ISBN 0-8229-3770-0 (cl.).—ISBN 0-8229-5515-6 (pbk.)
      I. Title.   II. Series.
PS 3558.A82316D66 1994   93-37786
811'.54—dc20   CIP

A CIP catalogue record for this book is available from the British Library.
Eurospan, London

The author and publisher wish to express their grateful acknowledgment to the following publications in which some of these poems first appeared: *Apalachee Quarterly* ("The Right Place for Love"); *Beloit Poetry Journal* ("Jean-Paul Sartre in the Bathtub"); *The Carleton Miscellany* ("Pessimism in a Burger King in Minneapolis," "My Brother's Face"); *Florida Review* ("Wallet," "Where John Berryman Jumped"); *The Georgia Review* ("Honeymoon," "The Prejohn," "T. S. Eliot's Dinners"); *Harvard Magazine* ("Sitting on the Porch with Mr. Schlessinger"); *Kayak* ("Allende, Allende," "The Revolution in Oakland"); *The Madison Review* ("Ears"); *the minnesota review* ("The Complaint of a Househusband," "Divorce," "Eduardo Mondlane," "The Havana Psychiatric Hospital," "The Invisible Hand," "My Wife's Shoes," "New York"); *New Collage Magazine* ("Frogs," "Swing"); *New Delta Review* ("Jogging at Dusk," "My Garden at Night"); *Poetry* ("My Cat Jack"); *Poetry Durham* ("Eeyore's Tail," "My Freshman Year," "Tee-Ball"); *Poetry Northwest* ("Fifteen Hungry Cheerleaders"); *Snake Nation Review* ("The Civil War," "Quality Time"); *Southern Poetry Review* ("Penguins," "Water Fear"); *The Southern Review* ("Mourning the Dying American Female Names," "My Neighbor's Pants," "My Vacuum Cleaner Suffers Remorse," "Pennies," "Pumpkin Lust"); *Sun Dog* ("Marriage," "Yeats's Grave"); *TriQuarterly* ("Lawn Fertilizer," "Male Grief"); *The Wormwood Review* ("Remembering the Tidy Town Laundromat," "We Buy Our Couch"); and *Yankee Magazine* ("Listening").

"My Cat Jack" was reprinted in *Writing: How and Why, Writing Poetry,* and *Diving for Poems.*

"Mourning the Dying American Female Names" was reprinted in *Anthology of Magazine Verse and Yearbook of American Poetry, A New Geography of Poetry,* and *North of Wakulla: An Anhinga Anthology.*

"The Prejohn" was reprinted in *Keener Sounds: Selected Poems from the Georgia Review.*

Book Design: Frank Lehner

For my family:
Ted, Hermione, Bob,
Elaine, Bernadette,
Sam, and Molly

III. Not Maddened by Domesticity

I

HOME THOUGHTS

SITTING ON THE PORCH WITH MR. SCHLESSINGER

He flings his cigarette through the evening air
to the lawn where it slowly fades.
Inside, the TV he left to sit with me
plays an Orioles game, Gus Triandos at bat.
His wife is in the kitchen making crab soup.
Today, he jokes, a neighbor asked to borrow
his "paramour." I can't think of anything
funny to say, or anything at all.
Half of last night I spent fooling with the clasp
of his daughter's bra in Dunbarton Park.
The softness of her breasts amazes me
even though my mind watches everything I do.
I ask myself if he'd hate me if he knew.
His long, yellow fingers fumble in his Camels pack.
Julie says he's disappointed with his life
because he never got to use his brains.
He's been building kitchen cabinets
since he was my age. When I begin to tell him
about my literature courses at school,
he notices the sidewalk needs to be fixed.
Since the neighborhood started changing,
no one keeps up their property anymore.
I promise myself I'll get rich somehow
and buy a house in a fancy suburb without sidewalks
where he will have a room.
His two oldest children have already married non-Jews.
I don't think he would hate me.
Blue TV light flickers through an upstairs window.

Our shirts are sticking to our chests.
Reaching in my pocket, I say
I have something I'd like him to read.
It is my "story" about my grief and shame
when my father drank himself to death.
He disappears into the kitchen for better light.
Fifteen minutes later his wife, in tears,
comes out in her apron and embraces me.

SWING

Like a row of black hinges, rusty ventricles,
the bankers' patent-leather shoes started to tap
when Benny Goodman jumped "Sing, Sing, Sing"
at Carnegie Hall four years before the war.
It was "jungle music," the force
of something remembered. Once my Dad told me
no son could accomplish as much as his father:
"Whoever heard of George Washington's boy?"
He had founded Happy Hawkins and His Nighthawks,
toured Europe three times, introduced jazz
to Switzerland. A drunken recital, this story repeated
like a beating heart. In the late thirties my parents
went to New York, danced to Tommy Dorsey and
        Artie Shaw.
Harry James's trumpet pumped the air as bands
coalesced and dissolved, then Glenn Miller's
USO plane went down over the Channel. Only later
did I think to ask, "What about Washington's *father*?"
On my last visit to San Francisco in 1963,
my Dad's saxophone lay on a shelf, tarnished green,
reed missing, pads dry, holes like little windows
into the absent column of breath. I wonder, though,
if they're still bopping in Switzerland
because once heard, my Dad always said,
the music can never be forgotten.

UNCLE

I remember him even now
as a sunny man who loved sweet corn
and showed me how he got the water boiling
before taking his basket to the garden.
He was a high-school principal,
a fiddler and square-dance caller who sang
"head for the hole in the old dishpan"
until all the couples came right again.
But surgery took half his esophagus
and chemotherapy turned him yellow.
He had to eat pureed corn
through a hole cut below his ribs.
Then my aunt caught him
in the pantry buttoning his shirt
and re-screwing the cap on the gin.
He went to Philadelphia to see *Deep Throat*
and announced, "They showed everything,"
but I believe he began to see
something they couldn't show.
The hospital ran a string down his nose
to keep his pharynx from closing.
Next he kicked my overweight aunt
out of the bedroom and brought
the neighbor's widow in.
"What's to stop me," he asked.
When he finally died, I remembered
how he had stood by my father's grave,
offering to do whatever he could.
But there wasn't anything.

FROGS

My stepfather, the Franklin County doctor,
liked to tell the story of how one night
he went frog-catching with the funeral director,
shining their lights into the dark pond.
Since they returned home a little drunk
and it was a cool place, they hung their lumpy bag
in Jake Minnich's mortuary only to find next morning
dozens of frogs escaped among the corpses
like bouncing green glands.
Days later they were still finding them
tucked in the satin linings of the caskets.
I knew he wished he had more such stories
because they showed he was one of the boys,
but he wasn't. Something made him awkward.
One October years later when we buried him,
his born-again daughter refused to show.
His suspicious son, the furniture salesman,
checked to make sure the grave
had the waterproof liner we'd paid for.
And I was noticing how the unchilled inner leaves
of the maple I stood under were still green
while the outer ones had turned yellow
like the older generation falling away.
I suppose I neglected him
as much as the others, but at least now
I can't think of myself laid out
without remembering those frogs.

SKATING

In the dank, gray, cinder block roller-rink,
their chrysalis, the subteens swarm.
The "cute" boy, shirttails flying, speeds
through a chain of four girls, breaking
their grip, rough, producing loads of giggles,
the minds of all dark but knowing somehow
of the fantastic change about to come.
The rental skates are tough as army boots,
sweat-stained uppers, polyurethane wheels chipped
by generations probably going back to Plato.
Here and there a few adults skate,
mostly propping up smaller children
as mares nuzzle their foals to stand, but
I notice one gray-haired man with a woman,
his daughter, fighting. Is she deaf? Retarded?
She can't speak. He has the exasperated
look of a man life has called to be a saint
when he didn't really feel like it.
He should be thinking retirement, trips
to Hawaii, but instead has to worry how
this daughter will survive when he ceases to be.
She is pale, unnaturally. Skinny. She waves
freckled stick arms in his face, demanding
God knows what, until he sits on a bench,
crosses his legs, his mind rolling over
some hard floor of knowledge.
Finally she gives up, moves into the
careening crowd—but she is brilliant,
cruising smoothly among the subteenagers,

on the turns laying one foot over the other
like jumping checkers, sure, relaxed
from a lifetime of weekly outings. When
she passes his sullen bench, she waves
to her Dad, but as she circles, her hands
linger strangely by her face, a palm
by each cheek, fluttering spasmodically
like a butterfly trying to be born.

THE PREJOHN

Last night at the movie theater,
going to relieve myself,
I kept thinking what a hard day
Adam must have had
when he was obliged to name all those animals:
kangaroo, porcupine, protozoa, drosophila, and on
        and on.
That must be why so many things
remain unnamed;
for example, the little room you enter
before you get to the bathroom.
I paused there, puzzled, pondering—
and hoping no one would come in and get the wrong
        impression.
What's the purpose of this room? You say
it's so outsiders of the different gender
don't catch any untoward sights,
but clearly we don't need a whole room for that—
just a crook or partition.
Why have prejohns
when we don't have precars or prekitchens?
I examined the room carefully.
It had bright lights, flowered wallpaper, white moldings.
I've had friends who lived in worse places than this!
And think of the thousands of prejohns across the country,
empty, going to waste.
We should at least put in shelves
and use them to store jams and jellies.
Or they could house refugees

from countries less fortunate and democratic than our own.
Or we could chain a prisoner in each one.
That way, not only would we relieve prison overcrowding,
but we'd provide a warning against crime
to every citizen going to take a whiz.
But something's wrong here.
It's the room itself we should get rid of.
We've all become Greta Garbos
in our quest for privacy.
We've become islands, not part of the main.
Why do we even need a bathroom
to go to the bathroom?
Shouldn't we be more like Adam's animals,
innocent and free, urinating in the wind,
defecating in the fields,
returning what we don't need
to great Nature from which it came?
O, yes, yes, shouldn't we be more like the French?

MOURNING THE DYING AMERICAN FEMALE NAMES

In the Altha Diner on the Florida panhandle
a stocky white-haired woman
with a plastic nameplate "Mildred"
gently turns my burger, and I fall into grief.
I remember the long, hot drives to North Carolina
to visit Aunt Alma, who put up quarts of peaches,
and my grandmother Gladys with her pieced quilts.
Many names are almost gone: Gertrude, Myrtle,
Agnes, Bernice, Hortense, Edna, Doris, and Hilda.
They were wide women, cotton-clothed, early rising.
You had to move your mouth to say their names,
and they meant strength, spear, battle, and victory.
When did women stop being Saxons and Goths?
What frog Fate turned them into Alison, Melissa,
Valerie, Natalie, Adrienne, and Lucinda,
diminished them to Wendy, Cindy, Suzy, and Vicky?
I look at these young women
and hope they are headed for the presidency,
but I fear America has other plans in mind,
that they be no longer at war
but subdued instead in amorphous corporate work,
somebody's assistant, something in a bank,
single parent with word-processing skills.
They must have been made French
so they could be cheap foreign labor.
Well, all I can say is,
Good luck to you

Kimberly, Darlene, Cheryl, Heather, and Amy.
Good luck April, Melanie, Becky, and Kelly.
I hope it goes well for you.
But for a moment let us mourn.
Now is the time to say good-bye
to Florence, Muriel, Ethel, and Thelma.
Good-bye Minnie, Ada, Bertha, and Edith.

PENNIES

In the 7-11 I buy milk,
get three cents back and wonder:
what can I make of my change,
the three dark spots in my palm.
Once these well-muscled citizens
did the nation's work: they were sunburnt
Scotch-Irish plowing Nebraska, sooty Welshmen
descending the coal mines of Pennsylvania,
African ex-slaves picking Alabama's cotton.
They were round and carried on their backs
the bearded, warty face of a president
who believed in government of, by, and for
the people. Now they are nothing,
the empty hoof-marks of an economy
which has galloped away.
What happened to sweated labor?
Doesn't anyone make anything any more?
Our thoroughbred corporations just
throw them aside. They fill jars
on bedroom bureaus, piled roughly
in miserable ghettoes.
They sit idly in cups next to
cash registers with signs saying:
"Got one, leave one; need one, take one."
They have been replaced by silver-colored money:
aristocratic Kennedy half-dollars,
fat bourgeois quarters, little yuppie dimes,
ever anxious lower-middle class nickles.

O poor pennies! Displaced workers! Despised citizens!
All you are good for now is
to litter the bottoms of wishing wells
and to cover the eyes of the dead.

GOING TO FLORIDA

One photo caught us in Williamsburg
in the wooden stocks, faces smiling,
butts sticking out: Bob, me, Mother, Betty.
The "genuine" blacksmith made the lock.
Betty was the first woman
I remember seeing naked, sitting in the bathroom,
her scrawny hip strangely blue.
Another photo has us punting through the swamps
of South Carolina, shouting "Chloe!"
I've lost the reason why.
After thirty years memory fades,
like the photos, is the photos mostly.
Bob and I were only teenagers.
In Florida finally we ate oranges
from the trees; smudge pots kept them warm.
At the track in Miami a red circle
of phony hydrants lightened the dogs.
Bright birds adorned Betty's
cruciform arms at "Parrot Jungle."
Years later Mother told us
Betty propositioned her on that trip.
More years later Betty's own memory
came apart, then came strangely alive.
Her dead parents scolded her, kept scolding her
for what she had become.
Finally in order to keep them quiet,
all alone in Baltimore,
she put a shotgun in her mouth.

My Freshman Year

In fall, the junior I wanted to be
practiced wheelies in the parking lot,
his gleaming blue Triumph absorbing every shock.
In winter, said the blond boy's poem,
the campus became an ashtray.
We had bunks in rooms meant for valets.
My roommate, a future dentist,
kept his desk lamp on night and day,
trying to sprout peas.
All he ever produced was a plate of dirt.
When Russian ships approached Cuba,
my classmates steamed off to the women's colleges,
convinced the world was about to end,
or at least hoping
the girls would see it that way.
At our mixer, Bo Didley sang "I'm a Man."
Now I grow alarmed to find my class
sliding slowly forward in the Alumni magazine—
prospering, spawning, remarrying, whatever.
I can no longer remember most of them,
but I can still see the eyes
of the mother of the blond boy
when she asked us to be kind to him
because he was sicker than he knew.

YEATS'S GRAVE

I rented a tiny Morris Minor in Galway
and drove north toward Sligo,
thinking how when they dug you up in France,
they must have dug up the monkey-glands too.
Ah, Willie, you had more balls than me.
I would have been scared of the operation
and would have lain awake nights,
fearing fur covering my body
and some bottomless craving for bananas.
But it worked pretty well for you,
throwing you in a fury onto George
and the bodies of various other ladies,
perhaps imagining them as six-foot redheads
but nonetheless achieving an acceptance
of their imperfect flesh.
Somewhere in wild Connemara
I picked up a hitchhiking couple,
a French girl and an Egyptian,
who had never heard of you.
Crammed in the Morris, they attempted
to render your poems into Arabic.
When I told them
you had once wished to exist outside of time
but had become monkey-wise,
they decided to come with me
to visit your grave.

So we finally stood in the rain
in Drumcliffe churchyard under Ben Bulben
reading your terse inscription:

> *Cast a cold eye*
> *On life, on death.*
> *Horseman, pass by!*

I picked up a handful of gravel
and wondered if only through embracing this earth
could we reach such austerity—
while the French girl asked me,
"Was he famous?"

Jean-Paul Sartre in the Bathtub

"I took this bath consciously,
excluding all alternatives,
and knowing full well
that no one else
could take it for me."

Sartre turns the spigot for more hot water.

"The tub, though, does not care
who uses it. It was made
for anyone."

Sartre reaches for the soap.

"Even so, I do not become related
with the others who might have
used it. The tub denies
my individuality without
putting me in community."

Sartre washes his legs.

"The act of bathing, however,
is my own. Therefore I regain
myself in an indifferent tub."

Sartre gets out of the tub and
dries himself, happy for being
Sartre again after
a difficult bath.

My Brother's Face

My brother's face is
polished by sleep.
His red beard and hair
glisten on the pillow.
Outside his window
a mockingbird jumps and sings
in the banana tree.
The first gleaming trucks
change gears uphill
on California Highway 1
and leave pieces of smoke
in the sky.
The morning light is
so clear.
Why are people born?
Why do people have faces?
The ocean is there
with its shining water.
The border of morning light
is moving gradually west
as the earth
rolls toward the sun.

THE REVOLUTION IN OAKLAND

Lucy filled the closet with pamphlets.
Jum and Winston refused to be housebroken.
Every night Lucy toked up on the penis pipe.
Our days were smoke.
Using piss from a pregnant friend,
Rory got on welfare.
Aggie slept in the backyard.
She found beauty in the decrepit house.
She wanted to feel right.
Something was stirring in the rented houses of the Bay Area.
The People's Peace Treaty. Produce Conspiracy.
Alex told us about the thirties.
His wife was dead. He cried.
The Brigade returned from Cuba,
smoking cigars.
I tried to write.
I wanted women to manage my feelings.
Aggie said I wasn't bad.
It's all right to cry.
We were trying to change ourselves.
Drinking Regal Beer,
we planned a garden, never planted.
Auto mechanics. First Aid.
We talked about Diana Oughton,
blown apart by her own bomb in New York.
The papers said her problems were personal.
Lucy said society was bad.
We learned karate.

Aggie said we were damaged inside,
we couldn't feel right.
Rory was caught shoplifting.
The stores were our enemy.
Packaging was bad.
Aggie cut off all her hair.
An apartment complex fills the lot
where our house once stood.
In 1970 we came apart.

The Survivalist

His Spanish was good, but not
enough to understand when Maria asked
his pretty wife why she'd married him,
which made him mad. He explained, hands
patting his flannel shirt front, how
he'd built the three-foot thick walls,
the odd-shaped stones flying to their places
once he relaxed his mind. Everything
they had came from the dump, even the shirt.
"Look, this stereo can play this Sinatra record.
This rifle fires, why would anyone toss that."
They raised grunty pigs, grew vegetables
in the bright New Mexican sun, depended
on no one, but had no cash for dental work.
She'd have to lose some teeth. "Looks aren't
everything. The house can take a hit almost."
She answered that when they met he knew somehow,
not about the wreck which killed her parents, the semi
shearing their car, but about her dream every night
of the bloody heads calling her name.

SWISS ARMY MIDLIFE CRISIS

On the snowy border passes of a country
which never fights, the soldiers pass their time
inventing multiple-use objects.
Propping their halberds against boulders
and pulling their camp stools in a circle,
sitting with pantaloons puffing about posteriors,
they recall past triumphs. The famous knife,
of course, with its corkscrew and tweezers,
but also the Swiss Army Pipe, which besides
producing puffable smoke, can pound in tent pegs.
"This is not a pipe!" Staff Sergeant Hans jests
while demonstrating its use as a tiny periscope.
Next, the Swiss Army Kite covered with stickum
catches flies; then flying becomes a billboard
puffing Swiss produce; finally, hauled in, it
serves as a somewhat tacky hammock. And lastly
the Swiss Army Dictionary: unlike its impoverished
cousins which only define words by one another,
it has an actual sample object for each entry
which may be prized out like the knife's awl.
Vaguely, however, Hans, just turned forty-five,
senses his life has gone Swiss amiss.
Hearing Helga yodeling down the valley,
thumping at her prized butter churn, he ruefully
muses, "Might I not also have been an English Rex?
And a Raoul romancing Veronica and Rosa?
And a Tex lassoing big broncos?
Why, O why have I spent my life becoming
this one-and-only Swiss Army Hans?"

HONEYMOON

When we pick up our marriage license,
the Commonwealth of Pennsylvania, full of wisdom,
gives us a plastic bag of promotional gifts
deemed useful to wedded life:
a roll of Tums, a bottle of Windex, two dozen aspirin.
As we drive to the Delaware coast,
my wife finds the true treasure
nestled at the bottom of the bag,
a paperback picturing a dark-haired girl on a cliff,
her white dress blowing in the wind, *The Zephyrs of Love.*
For the next two days we hardly leave the room.
We don't even bother to dress.
Instead we take turns reading the book aloud.
It seems the poor English girl, Dominique,
was forced to marry a Greek shipping tycoon
with a scar across his face
because her father owed him lots of money.
She hated Petros with his arrogant ways
and ugly disfiguration
until one night he slipped into her room.
Slowly he ran his swarthy hand
under Dominique's satin nightgown.
When she woke to protest,
he shouted, "But you're my wife!"
As Dominique struggled futilely,
an animal passion seized her soul.
My wife and I stare at each other,
then at my scars:
the knee with the cartilage operation

and the finger I cut on a beer can.
We've taken years to decide to marry,
and we're still not completely sure.
How do Dominique and Petros do it?
They quickly resolve all their differences
as Petros forgives her father's debt
and reveals he received his scar
fighting the Nazis in the Resistance.
Our honeymoon is over.
I think my wife and I are ready
for the Windex, Tums, and aspirin,
knowing our lives will never shine
with the wonderful light of inevitability.
That's all right.
As we take a last walk down the beach,
I practice shouting, "But you're my wife!"

MARRIAGE

When my wife tells me
her parents are coming to visit for a month,
I begin to think of asexual reproduction,
of dusky potatoes
deep under ground,
each self-sufficient in its jacket,
slowly protruding ghostly tubers,
of hydra budding under cool blue water,
of red sparkling strawberries
weaving nets of wiry runners,
of dank mushrooms casting spores,
of humble amoebae splitting softly in two.
And I think how in forsaking love,
these mitotic creatures have escaped so much,
not in the least dying,
their very flesh
persisting through the generations.
But that night beside me on the bed,
my wife lies asleep,
her hair across her neck.
I remember how she first taught me
the buttery smell of sheets
hung in the sun to dry.
And I watch as the moon streaming through the window
turns her face to pure light.

Where John Berryman Jumped

In the sun the broken ice
standing in the river
sends up thick frayed strings.
A bulldozer on the bank
pushes coal about.
Standing on the bridge
I can see my little shadow
wriggling in the water.
The only words in sight
stick to a dark brick building:
St. Mary's Hospital.
I heard Berryman once in Cambridge.
His songs carried bourbon
even twenty rows back.
Waving his arms at us,
he recited all the woes of Henry,
and nearly fell off the stage.
It was his dead father's pull.
I know.
And I wonder what it's like,
the dark place with no words.
Can you go uninjured there?
Those tassels growing from the ice
look so loose and soft.
I wish I knew
what they're called.
Berryman put his leg over this rail,
waved to passing students, and leapt.
I look around. No one there.
So I begin to sing.

II

THE RIGHT PLACE FOR LOVE

THE RIGHT PLACE FOR LOVE

Earth's the right place for love:
I don't know where it's likely to go better.
—Robert Frost, "Birches"

Waiting for a friend in his Arlington kitchen,
drinking flown-in Coors,
I imagine that I could love the little boy,
open-spined from birth,
strapped to a skateboard like a beggar,
who beams when he hears
his Daddy's motorcycle roaring in the drive.
My friend has a double bourbon
in a heavy Russian glass.
They think the microwaves at the Moscow embassy
might have done it, but no one really knows.
The next day we cross the Potomac
in the gritty chill of winter
to buy some light tanks for Pakistan.
My friend hates the paperwork,
trudging from the Pentagon to the White House,
arranging for Germany to be the front.
On Avenue C outside the State Department,
winos sleep on the hot air grates.
Petitioners with relatives trapped in the Ukraine
sit on lawn chairs, waving signs.
In the lobby my friend asks me—
even though I've only been married for a month—
if I've ever considered divorce.
I say I guess I have.

When we shake hands, I avoid his eyes
and look past him at a lighted glass case.
It has a collection of tiny, wooden horses
and a large, blue map
showing the countries of our world.

NEW YORK

At night the bag ladies bed down
on benches in Needle Park.
They have millions, people say,
stashed somewhere, but prefer
to live this way.
The heavy lady nearest me
takes off her shoes,
puts her bag beneath her head.
Her ear is full of clotted blood.
Fine grit rains down on us
from the summer sky.
Earlier, on Fifth Avenue,
I saw a man drop dead.
People walked around him
where he lay.
I too was scared.
Maybe it was a trick.
Maybe he'd jump up with a gun.
Finally the policeman who came
said it was just a heart attack.
My tourist book says one hundred years ago
this land was all dairy farms
down to 42nd Street
Near my hotel a man
pushes against the walls.
"The buildings are sliding
into the river," he says.
"Don't worry," is all I can reply.
"Just don't worry."

EAST RIVER PRISON BARGE

The powerboats cut the water
like long, white knives. Beefy men,
some too young you'd think to afford
the pop, steer from perches
while even younger women catch
the sun. Past Roosevelt Island,
the town houses in the fifties
with their leafy trees. They favor
naughty names: Hooky, Delinquent,
Renegade. Near Manhattan Bridge
they pass the barge, gray, five stories,
rolls of razor wire atop chicken mesh
where inmates hang, blots on graph paper,
all black and brown men yelling
what they'd do with the playgirls' holes.
The diesel roar drowns them out.
"No Docking!" says the sign. Shining in the light,
the cruisers round the Battery, head for the Narrows,
escape for their long weekends.

Eduardo Mondlane

President of Frelimo, the Front
for the Liberation of Mozambique

There was a Frelimo funeral nearly every month
in Dar es Salaam.
I remember the middle-aged white lady
who requested a scotch-and-soda,
then argued that Albert Schweitzer
hadn't done any good.
Perhaps we should have resisted
when the Institute asked us
to show their film on democracy.
My students said they liked the idea,
but the day the World Court ruled
South Africa could keep Namibia,
they stood around their radios weeping.
All night the palm trees rattled,
and the old hippo coughed down in the bay.
The head of the Institute flew out from New York
just to say we were in the "vortex of History."
But Mondlane said our relation was "vitiated."
He lectured us like the professor he used to be,
his voice booming around the room.
The students shouldn't be Westernized;
they had to be taught to sacrifice.
The friendly headmaster, who had his T-bird
shipped in from Laos, tried to get books.
For half an hour every morning

the rain pounded so hard classes had to stop.
We were doing our best.
The white lady was kind enough
to lend her cottage to Mondlane to work in.
But when he opened the package postmarked "Moscow,"
the explosion knocked down the mailman
who was already a block away.

THE HAVANA PSYCHIATRIC HOSPITAL

The VA administrator from Seattle is pleased that
the rugs in the old Havana Hilton stink,
crippled Fords and Studebakers leak blue smoke,
Avenida Salvador Allende is pocked with holes.
We have come to visit the house of the crazy people,
casa de dementes, where they see a world I fear.
How patiently the tiny women make paper flowers
while the man in the barber's chair jumps back, screaming.
Before and After photos in the lounge show Batista's days:
naked men and women with open sores squat in cages.
The head of St. Elizabeth's Hospital gets suspicious.
These patients are too clean. Dr. Eduardo Ordaz
explains that, down from the mountains,
they wished first to save the most wretched.
Then medicines were embargoed, even tranquilizers.
What the man in the barber's chair must see is death,
walking with shining hands along the sunny corridor.
How long can idealism last? In a giant mural
in the Plaza de la Revolucíon, Che Guevara,
his face framed with curls, gazes at the empty sky.
The billboards say: *Los hombres mueren*
pero la patria vive para siempre.
I wish to see only what is really there.
Are we each alone?
The VA man is delighted to find the stores under-stocked,
pants rationed, paint peeling off the houses.
He says even tobacco has to be imported.

He tells us the docks are crowded
with young men who want to get out.
I see them myself.
They are healthy
and strong, their faces
bright with the dream of Miami.

THE INVISIBLE HAND MEETS THE DEAD HAND

HIGH ABOVE WASHINGTON, D.C.

There! in the clouds can't you see
the Invisible Hand prancing, tumbling?
It soars over the Reflecting Pool,
pirouettes atop the Washington Monument.
I think it must be Adam Smith's,
the Hand he said would harmonize
all selfish interests, miraculously making whole
a society of pure individuals. Down on the ground
thousands of portly men wearing Adam Smith ties
adore this Hand as they circle the obelisk,
their hair slicked back and their flies open.
Then suddenly they squat, the flesh of their
upper arms quivering, and in unison croak:
"Ketchup is a vegetable! No new taxes!"
I figure them to be fiscal conservatives
because they set out buckets full of loopholes
into which they piss, claiming confirmation
of the trickle-down theory. Next they chant:
"Death to welfare queens! Send in the Marines!"
With arm gestures, they indicate their belief
that government should be small, but the army big
because democracy must be defended even in
caliphates. And what is the Dead Hand doing here,
this skeletal yellow apparition? O, it just came
to party. It chases the Invisible Hand, busy dancing
in the sky like Mickey Mouse's immaculate glove.
They clasp, shake, high five, then start to tango.

Pessimism in a Burger King in Minneapolis

Last night my TV showed me Africa:
a wildebeest circling fretfully
while three hyenas ate its belly.
Sour Schopenhauer told us to compare
the little joy of the eaters
with the big unhappiness of the eaten
to see what our world is.
Wasn't civilization smart
to make food a comedy?
Three-color pictures on the wall:
smiling hot dogs boogaloo
with french fries wearing sundresses.
Mr. Milkshake and Mrs. Coleslaw
plan a pleasant weekend
in my tummy.
I stare at my hamburger calmly,
wondering where it came from.
Fuzzy thoughts of Nebraska feedlots
filter through my head.
Suppose the contents of this bun
were really someone's mother.
Should I be like Gandhi
and strain my water through a napkin?
My hunger nearly makes me cry.
How I wish we could all be angels
without stomachs,
but heaven is so far away.
Lifting my burger to my face,
I decide to embrace the tragedy of life
and take a bite.

T. S. Eliot's Dinners

Let us try to imagine for a moment
all of T. S. Eliot's dinners
lined up side by side on Interstate 10.
There they are—27,831 of them
stretching 5½ miles on the gravel shoulder
from Exit 2 nearly to Exit 3.
We see the progression from his baby gruel
to his adult repasts.
There's the Stilton cheese
he felt he had to stay in England for.
There are all the peaches he dared to eat—
a total of seven.
And there's the melba toast
Valerie had to feed him in his declining years.
From the surrounding fields
cows nuzzle forward to the fences,
staring at the steaks, roasts, and ribs.
They must feel proud of the contribution
their kinfolk made
to the articulation of the waste land.
Then, as I'm standing there,
a highway patrolman stops, a big-gutted redneck
who asks, "What's that you've got there, boy?"
When I tell him it is all of T. S. Eliot's dinners,
he falls back in abashed awe
and quotes a line of Dante's *Inferno*
in the original Italian:

> *per la dannosa colpa della gola,*
> *come tu vedi, all pioggia mi fiacco*

which he proceeds to translate:
        for the damning fault of gluttony,
        as you see, I lie helpless in the rain.
It's perfectly sunny,
but hearing barking, I look up and see
a three-headed dog
snarling in the front seat of his squad car.
So I attempt to comfort him by saying,
"Don't take it so hard, Bubba.
Eating's not evil. It can't be."
But Bubba only blubbers.
He gestures along the road with his revolver:
"What's all this mess then?"
Now's my chance.
I raise my arms jubilantly high.
"Don't you worry none, Bubba.
This here's God's message to us
that we're supposed to cherish Creation
and eat it.
You see, Old Possum stopped loving life
so God punished him
by not letting him take his dinners with him.
It's plain as day."
I lower my arms. When Bubba smiles,
I know I've saved a soul.

THE COMPLAINT OF A HOUSEHUSBAND

Your colleagues ignore me.
When I hysterically insist on talking,
they turn to you.
All my thoughts have suddenly become opinions.
Why have I hung my Ph.D. in the bathroom?
My days just simply disappear.
I can't even remember this morning
except "Search for Tomorrow."
Alone with the dog,
I eagerly await your return at dusk,
as if you were reality itself,
only to find your life is names
I barely know.
You demand sympathy
because they look down on you
for being a woman.
And my sympathy has increased
along with my dependence.
The stairs grow dustballs
the way a garden makes cabbages.
I roam from room to room,
looking for things to pick up,
and scream at the milk carton
you left on the counter.
When I say I've developed "dishpan penis,"
you forget to laugh.

My mother asks who sleeps on top.
We are forging ahead
toward a new relationship,
but the road is dense.
Twenty minutes before the guests arrive,
I nervously scrub the toilet bowl.

My Vacuum Cleaner Suffers Remorse

After a strenuous afternoon cleaning house,
my vacuum cleaner is still going strong.
Not only is it working harder than ever,
but it is blaming itself
for the existence of dirt.
Checking its plate, I see it was made in Boston.
Taking pity, I tell it to lighten up.
After all, it's living in Florida now
where people indulge themselves
in all sorts of crazy things.
I tell it about my pal Lance down in Miami
who gave his cocker spaniel herpes
but didn't feel a twinge of conscience
since medical science is sure to find a cure soon.
My vacuum cleaner, however, remains upright,
insisting that the progress of Western Civilization
depends on a sense of guilt.
After all, weren't clocks invented by medieval monks
who had to get up for matins
to cleanse themselves from original sin.
Then Europe inched forward
on the backs of black-cloaked merchants
denying themselves pleasures,
accumulating pennies,
thereby showing themselves among the Elect.
Finally, the Industrial Revolution
raised itself on the shoulders of pious workers
willing to endure sixteen-hour days
in return for their heavenly reward.

"But this is nonsense!" I shout. "Don't you know
we've gotten past that?" And I explain
how in Post-Industrial Society
consumption is the problem rather than production.
"Really you're more important now as a commodity
than as a cleaning instrument."
But my vacuum cleaner doesn't agree.
It stubbornly digs in its rollers, pouts,
and refuses to relinquish its remorse.
So finally, to humor it, I give in.
"OK," I say, "if that's the way you feel,
let's go ahead and do the drapes."

Remembering the Tidy Town Laundromat

Machinery has driven us bozo, that's clear.
Why else would every house in this neighborhood
have a washer-drier used just four hours a week?
We all look normal enough, in our clean outfits,
but we've lost the guts to wash together.
I remember my old laundromat in Palo Alto.
It was easy enough, I tell you,
to learn not to put your hand
in the Speedqueen with the spastic agitator.
Where else would I have met
the nice old lady
whose T-shirt read, "Sit on it!"
Where else would I have learned
the correct response to: "*Cochino,
deme todo su dinero, pronto!*"
And where else would I have become friends
with the man with half a face.
No more reaching under my chair
to find a petrified village of chewing gum.
No more notices of spaniels missing.
Good-bye to the coeds washing their underwear.
Wrongly have I cut myself off
from the dangerous and the grotesque
and the merely sexual.
Everybody where I live now
is too proper, I say.
Why can't we share our machines?

THE CIVIL WAR

Blue soldiers emerge from the trees
behind the barn, line abreast, and
march downhill under fire as if they
had no fear. The air turns so dark
with smoke from the Confederate cannon
by the creek that we hear the screams
but can't tell who fell. In their woolen suits
even the downed men must keep sweating.
Are they still listening, muttering
to themselves the reasons they perished?
The spectators, out from Washington
for the day, trample the farmer's corn,
set up camp stools, throw sandwich
bags on the battlefield. When the skirmish
is over, the dead arise, pack their gear
in pickups, and drive home. We stop at McDonald's
for Happy Meals for the kids, try to imagine life
as different. Outside semis pound past on I-81;
the late afternoon sun glints off tinted glass;
and we are locked tight as in a plastic bag.
Only the historic dead under the ground
at Gettysburg remain uncertain
how the battle turned out.

ALLENDE, ALLENDE

The morning we drive to the trail
the radio says you killed yourself.
In 1963 my father drank himself to death
in an apartment off Market Street.
One day he hid in his closet
while kids broke in and stole his television.
He kept a drawing of my mother
tacked inside the closet door.
As we hike to Sandpiper Lake
a line runs through my head.
Allende, Allende, el pueblo te defiende.

We have such small lives.
Elaine and I argue until she cries.
She wants marriage to be perfect.
I say it can't be,
but I don't really care.
At night we can't sleep and watch the stars.
We both believe death is darkness.
So did you.
Allende, Allende, el pueblo te defiende.

Above the timberline
the Sierras are bare granite
cut up by glaciers two million years ago.
Their beauty has nothing in it.
Elaine finds tiny things to name—
paintbrush, groundsel, fleabane.
When will people get better?

La Moneda is hit and burning.
Allende, Allende, el pueblo te defiende.

At home in Palo Alto we lie in bed,
almost in love.
The paper says
you had gunpowder on your hands.
It says maybe you died fighting.
I hope it's true
because outside it's empty night.
We hold each other.
Allende, Allende, el pueblo te defiende.

WE BUY OUR COUCH

Crazy Bargaining Eddie
cruises forward in Hush Puppies.
Veering between Elaine and me,
he displays "your tuxedo model,"
"your flamestitch loveseat,"
and "your sectional sofa."
When he tells the prices, I ask myself:
Has the Mafia grabbed the couch industry?
What are twenty yards of cloth
and a few boards worth?
But I can't make a couch,
and we have no place for friends to sit.
Elaine and I have fought for months
without guests.
Eddie asks, "You checked out the mall?
We beat Dayton's. Hundred bucks.
Same stuff exactly."
He's right, but I can see
he isn't happy.
He wishes he had a department store
so he could put his furniture
in delicate make-believe rooms
instead of shabby rows.
Besides, the nice stores make better dough.
Is it his fault
he's Crazy Bargaining Eddie?
He sits with me on an overstuffed green divan.
He knows I want to buy and get out.
But Elaine balks. These couches aren't right.

She has dreamed of having one
since she was a girl.
They mean something
I can't understand.
"We've looked long enough," I say.
Crazy Bargaining Eddie averts his eyes
while Elaine agrees.

I Like Little Worlds

In heavy rain at night
I like sitting in my Plymouth
as the windows are drowned
and the glowing radio
brings pop songs from strange places.
I like my cactus garden
with its gimcrack prospector
who never gets thirsty
and who would have to tramp miles
before standing perplexed at the table's edge.
I like *Moby-Dick*
because I can carry Queequeg,
Ahab, the whale, and the Pacific Ocean
with me in my car.
I get upset
when everyone but Ishmael
is killed at the end,
but I turn back fifty pages
and there they all are again.
Best of all, because smallest,
I like my paperweight,
which when shaken, sprinkles snow
on the cars, houses, gardens, and churches
of a perfect Austrian village.
Under such skies,
I would surely be safe.

DEFENDING MARRIAGE

When my friend defended marriage
by comparing it to a car with two engines,
I should have known he'd be divorced within a year.
Instead I had to compare marriage
to a camel with two humps—
one on Tuesday and one on Friday.
Then they invited us over to dinner,
but somehow we didn't fathom the little clues:
the double bourbons, the Doritos, the dust.
All of their conversation sloped toward matrimony,
and they seemed bent on outdoing each other
in defending it. Their arguments
galloped around the table like Shetland ponies.
Of course we noticed, but didn't seriously ask
why she cried in the kitchen, why he yelled
at her crying, why they needed
two TV's in the bedroom.
And why didn't we catch on?
When we finally heard in the grocery store
they had moved apart, my wife and I
looked at each other in surprise,
our eyes suddenly troubled,
and began to defend marriage.

The Family Man

He experiences loss at the periphery:
the inevitable disappearance of
bathing suits, goggles, and paper plates.
Holes open on every side
of income.
At night he thinks of generations
linking each to each
while the coughing house settles.
Squirrels scratch the roof.
He must not fall.
Even pleasure takes a toll.
The fat station wagon,
bathed in fumes,
makes the eight year old sick.
Hamburger smoke rises through the trees.
In the shallows,
the sun burns away Lake Ocklawaha.
Surrounded by a hundred families
he'll never see again,
he squeezes down anger
as his wife complains about her weight.
Looking at other women walking by,
he faces the danger
of knowing his discontent.
The family separates him from fear.
He dreams of being alone in high mountains,
of hearing, without intermediary,
cold wind
sweeping bare granite.

"Eunuch"

At the party Tom cornered me,
crouched, coiled his arm around mine,
then called Graham "a choirboy eunuch,"
so I peeked across the room at his lank
blond hair, freckled arms, hands
which I believe had not touched a woman ever
but now held a sweating gin-and-tonic.
At thirty-six he had his Burmese cats,
harpsichord, and a talkative mother to keep.
I wanted to leave, but Tom held tight,
muscular, black-haired, intent.
"Lust is the only thing which makes sex
beautiful," he said minutes later
with a knowing wink. And I could guess
he had known it as ugly, or maybe
just boring, this edgy ex-Catholic
father of three with an obliging wife.
Was that why Tom hated him?
How could a man make so much venom?
Because for Graham, who played Mass
every Sunday, sitting at the gleaming organ,
building chord upon chord,
it was meaningful, overwhelming,
too meaningful ever to be done.

DIVORCE

Sometimes I think they should have mated like horses,
suddenly, and without introducing themselves.
Instead they exchanged names,
and wanted to be meant for each other.
Thus they were perplexed when he started wiping off
the saliva of her morning kiss
and she began discussing the grocery list
in the middle of intercourse.
They didn't know what to do
when their bodies became so familiar
they lost track of who was which sex.
Whenever they bumped into each other in the small house,
they said "Hi!" and couldn't see the humor
when he started saying it like Donald Duck,
she like Lauren Bacall.
They gave each other the tail ends of their days,
somehow expecting this time to be bigger
than the long hours spent at work.
They got confused when she began calling
her job as a receptionist a "career."
She admitted she envied his profession,
but he claimed proctology wasn't so entertaining.
They both expected the baby to unite them,
but hadn't realized it would be too inexperienced
to tell them what to do.
Once they saw they were sinking,
they wanted to ask their parents for help,
but their parents were already divorced.
Not knowing where to turn,
they believed the book which said

making love in chains was a liberating experience.
Finally a counselor told them
they would have to work on it,
but they didn't understand
why they couldn't do the same work with anyone else.
All people became interchangeable.
They still thought love gave life its meaning,
but had no idea where love came from
and renewed the search for the perfect one.
With all their furniture spread on the lawn,
they argued over who would get the dog.
Hearing a tremendous commotion overhead,
they looked up.
Even the birds in the sky were fighting.

JOGGING AT DUSK

As the sun settles down, half my neighborhood
convenes to sweat on the local high-school track.
I trot along like the rest,
pondering the great democracy of exercise,
when suddenly I realize the gyrating fellow beside me
has turned his body into a machine
perfect for harvesting grapes.
As he leaves me behind, I busy myself
devising schemes to develop his commercial potential.
Now here comes a sunken-chested specimen,
sprinting on his tiptoes with a scissoring step
which convinces me fatherhood is out of the question.
I feel embarrassed,
knowing no other sport could claim such an individual.
But I foresee happiness for him:
he will marry a full-breasted dental assistant
and lap me twice in the next all-city race.
Every time the pregnant runner takes a step,
I cringe, fearing delivery on the asphalt,
but she bounds gamely on.
I prognosticate that her offspring
will only be happy sitting in washing machines.
Across the track an elephantine gentleman
advances with such small steps
that at first I think he is gummed to the ground.
He must believe this exercise will make him live forever,
but I fear it will work out otherwise.
Finally, I know that jogger in the white visor.
He is a lawyer who runs very shrewdly.

Each stride can be interpreted in two dozen ways
and retracted if necessary.
Trying to keep up with him, I realize
he has good wind and will go far,
but death will come suddenly one morning,
and he will be surprised by its vast irrevocability.
As all the neighbors strain around the oval,
night sifts down through the sky.
Soon I can no longer see the other runners,
but I retain a sense of surrounding motion,
and I can still hear the whispering of their nylon shorts
going *shish-shish*
even in the darkness.

HOLDING BERNADETTE

In a room without windows, my infant daughter
struggles in the underwater
glow of the bilirubin light.
She clutches my finger, opens muddy eyes,
and gives me a puzzled look.
The machines blink and sing. I have no answers.
Even with three tubes, she can't
get enough glucose. I feel ashamed
for all the gray mornings driving to work
when I've half-wished to get it over.
I tell her we'll go fishing,
then explain how fish are funny, slippery animals
who live in the Gulf, miles away.
Her stupid heart! It thinks it can save itself
by cutting off circulation to her limbs.
I want to save myself by turning away,
but Elaine insists we return at midnight
to hold Bernadette.
How could the pioneers have toiled across the plains,
leaving child after child under empty stones?
She breathes softly, holding on,
her heart beating with its savage wish.
I want to tell her
how I felt at home once
in a tent west of Morogoro in Africa.
Waking in late afternoon,
I saw far away across the savannah
a family of giraffes moving in golden light
with their awkward, watery gait.

The grass billowed so peacefully,
as if holding all the generations.
In the parking garage
Elaine and I look at each other.
What is there to say?
Beneath her blouse her breasts are bound
to stop the milk.

MALE GRIEF

In the pale after-Labor Day sun of Cape Cod
he sits on the dark grass in a weathered chair
reading *Black Elk Speaks* while his family
churns around him. I date his daughter
and for the first time have come to meet him,
but he keeps apart. We eat lobster,
then the men watch the Olympics on TV
while the women clean up. His daughter
teaches me to speak into his right ear
instead of the left, knocked cold
when he fell from a farm-horse as a boy.
I strain to imagine him at half his size,
waking in the chill Ohio dawn to milk the cows,
alone in the barn, steam floating from the bucket.
When I sit by myself on the rocky beach,
I wonder if men are somehow injured
in their ability to love.
Over the years I read his long, typed letters
which reveal nothing of how he feels.
I watch as he canes chairs, braids rugs,
and refinishes stands for his absent children.
I notice how he places himself at tables
so strangers won't know about the ear.
Until one morning I see him
at the end of a hospital corridor.
When he is told that his granddaughter has died,
he begins to cry as though he himself
were trying to become the baby who has gone.

III

NOT MADDENED BY DOMESTICITY

Apnea

My infant son, Samuel, sleeps in his crib,
hunched forward like a small Mohammedan,
while I watch in the dark room,
unable to sleep, listening to his breathing.
The doctors say we all stop many times
each night, but decide to start again.
Two miles away the trucks on the interstate
sizzle. I realize how hard it is
not to think of myself as watched,
if only by some small man inside my head
who keeps everything going. Does he have
a little cot in there, does he ever sleep?
Outside a confused mockingbird starts to sing
long before dawn. The furnace goes on and off,
keeping the house warm. A bit later
the refrigerator does the same, a countermove.
Samuel's chest keeps heaving. Maybe
the world just happens, but sometimes it doesn't.
I can see I will spend the rest of my life
hoping my son will want to breathe.

WATER FEAR

On Sunday afternoon
we walk out on the levees at St. Marks.
The alligators lie in the shallow water,
still and dark as big rocks,
but people say they can outsprint horses,
catch their legs and drag them under.
Elaine says that's ridiculous. So I ask her
why do I have this recurrent dream?
I emerge from the cabin door onto the bright deck
just in time to see our infant son
crawling toward the rail.
As he nears the edge,
I wish I had him on a leash.
He tumbles, falls five stories, and, tiny as a pebble,
disappears in the foam.
I think of Hart Crane. I rear like a horse.
I have to decide to jump.
At night, as the wedding-cake lights of our ship
disappear over the horizon,
I go into my son's room to listen to his breathing.
I think of how his cousin's stopped one dawn,
of how the father found the baby all cold and blue
and baptized her in the sink.
Then I picture my son at ninety,
white-haired, safe at last.
As we come closer,
the alligators slide into deeper water.
The smooth, blue surface

reflects a world of clouds
and cabbage palms and tall grass.
Warm sunlight pours down.
Elaine says it's lovely,
and it is.
Walking on ahead of me,
she carries the boy in a pack on her back.

LISTENING

The baby leans
and listens
to that ocean inside.
You hold him,
you can hear it
as the lions hear it
deep in the grass.
We tire ourselves out
swimming in the outside ocean
which we try to cross.
Listen—this is the strange love
for sounds
of all those helpless ones.
Don't you know an old person
who has heard
the collapse inward
of outer logs
falling to the fire?

FIFTEEN HUNGRY CHEERLEADERS

On the drive-in movie screen, the cheerleaders
wave from their shocking pink Chevy van.
They are totally ignorant of the homicidal octopus
who inhabited the first feature.
Wherever they go, it is hot and sunny.
Few clothes are needed. Like large flowers,
they urge on their team,
and are just the same as ordinary people,
except for their tremendous desire to please.
They never complain about the acts they must perform
to help Joey the quarterback throw more touchdown
        passes.
In fact, they take ravenous pleasure in any sort of flesh.
My wife, who prefers more plot in her movies,
says she is bored to death,
but I say wait a minute.
I am thinking about the
mess of tentacles
which engulfed the poor waitress
during her vacation in the Bahamas.
Why do I have the sinking feeling
that these generous women cannot escape unpunished?
The cheerleaders aren't dumb.
It turns out they all went to Radcliffe,
and two have doctorates in marine biology.
But for some reason their suspicions aren't aroused
when they stop for cheeseburgers
and even the low-angle camera reveals

the suction cup marks on top of the counter.
Nor do they notice the slithery sounds
coming from under their van in the parking lot.
I tell my wife to roll up her window,
but she misinterprets my intentions
and puts one hand on my knee.
When she starts to unbutton my shirt,
I feel an urgent desire,
but for what I do not know.

PENGUINS

My two-year-old son
stands on my feet, grabs my hands,
and I waddle him to bed.
Holding him in the dark,
I think of the Emperors,
how in March they watch the sun
take ever shorter hops across the horizon
until it is only night.
As the temperature falls,
the winds churn maniacally.
The females have already disappeared
into the krill-rich sea,
leaving behind their eggs.
The males roll the shells onto their feet,
cover them with belly-flaps,
and circle in a tortue.
Perhaps the first month isn't so bad.
They can be masculine and tell jokes:
"Did you hear the one about the seal
who lost his suitcase?"
But in the second month they begin to ask irritably:
"Where in hell did those women go anyway?"
And by the third it must cross their minds
they could pop the eggs like bubbles.
Starving, they have lost half their weight.
Their eyes have gone dull without light.
Still, they clamp their beaks,
shifting silently from foot to foot.
They have lost all conception of forward and back.
They no longer know what they are waiting for.
But they wait.
And wait and wait,
holding their eggs in the impossible night.

Ears

Once in Mankato, Minnesota, I saw men
piling their plates with mashed potatoes.
I was doing the same! Then I noticed their ears
matched their food perfectly.
Since then, I haven't taken ears seriously.
Just for hearing purposes, wouldn't
a pair of plain funnels have been better?
But these gnarled flesh-vegetables! Why?
I seize my infant daughter to study an ear.
The waxy ridges form two C's
overlapping at top but not at bottom
with a hyphen tucked inside.
Perhaps ears are really spare parts
for some convoluted internal organ
sewn on outside like extra buttons.
Or maybe they're a species of anemone
meant to remind us of our underwater origins.
They look something like the Roman Coliseum.
Peering in the folds, I search for
a tiny lion and some cowering Christians.
Or perhaps our ears are curled to suggest
we can only understand each other in twisty ways.
I recall Van Gogh used his as stationery.
Maybe ears are God's signature
scrawled on our heads illegibly
and twice for good measure.
Or it could be ears are a sign

of that inevitable crumpling
which awaits our entire unfortunate flesh.
I'm afraid I've gotten dizzy
thinking about this topic.
Wishing I had never visited Minnesota,
I clutch my daughter to my chest,
then kiss her strange little flaps.

Lawn Fertilizer

One sunny afternoon standing in my yard
discussing lawn fertilizer
while his wife unloads groceries from their car
my neighbor suddenly confides that he often masturbates
rather than taking the trouble to make love.
His lawn looks brown. It needs some 8-8-8.
I recommend Scott's,
but he cocks his canary-colored head,
looking oddly quizzical.
So I picture his wife and him
and myself and my wife
and our neighbors on the other side
and all of the nearby couples
each in a steamy little bedroom
separated by ten yards of improperly cared for lawn,
and say, "Yes . . . I guess . . . it doesn't seem . . . you
    know."
What is his collie doing in my azaleas!
I wish I were seventeen again.
Life has gotten so disappointing lately.
"And you?" he asks sharply. I watch his wife,
still pretty, good legs,
hauling large bags of celery into the house.
One hundred years ago this hill would have been jungle,
full of animals with little regard for one another,
including us if we had been there.
And that's why it's so important
we fulfill our duties to suburban civilization.
So I smile at my neighbor encouragingly:
"Take the trouble, George. Take the trouble.
And for God's sake do something about your lawn."

MY WIFE'S SHOES

Chasing my errant cat one sloppy afternoon,
I unexpectedly find myself crawling
into my wife's closet, all alien and pink.
Cat gone. Nightgowns tickling my neck.
I start to leave, then spot her aluminum shoe rack
like a huge immigrant ship entering New York harbor,
the sturdy, honest couples lining the decks.
So many, so many! How will I ever clothe and feed them?
All my favorites are here: her saddle shoes from the
    eighth grade,
the blue sling-backs she wore on our first date in
    San Francisco,
the red pumps I removed the night of the big snow,
innocently to inquire which piggy had roast beef.
Ah, these shoes are as fertile as foreigners,
but they are so appallingly ignorant,
simple peasants come to the land of division of labor.
They have no skills. They will end up like Sacco and
    Vanzetti.
I think of my own closet.
Maybe the cat has gone there.
It is a humble closet, only three pairs of shoes,
but this pink closet is a tenement.
How will I ever satisfy my wife's lust for shoes?
They are not mere foot-coverings.
They have a religious significance like Veronica's
    handkerchief,
promising relief from this tawdry life.
Where do they come from anyway?
Over the seas. I picture a crew of small men,

singing in Norwegian, wearing stocking caps.
They trudge over the tundra,
rounding up tiny herds of shoe-shaped animals.
Then they patiently shuck the skins.
It is very difficult for us to envision,
but that is the fault of the division of labor
which has kept us apart for so long.
As a poet, my job is to imagine things;
I am never supposed to touch leather.
The shoe hunters may seem like foreigners,
but under the skin we are all really brothers and sisters.
This is proved by the exchange of commodities.
Hush, I think my wife is coming.
She mustn't find me like this in her closet.
Here is my poem. I think it is finished.
Quick! Give me your shoes!

QUALITY TIME

A stranger has entered my house
to take all my money, but has no tools
and seems intent on waking me up.
As the clock strikes four,
I am trying to get the diaper pail
open with one hand. Whew!
At last she falls asleep,
and I lower her gently as a watch spring
until she touches the crib. Instantly she flies up.
What a voice! We recommence parading.
When my well-off friends
talk about "quality time," I imagine them
home with their children discussing Descartes,
but as I walk, a stream of drool
runs along my collarbone, then cascades into my PJs.
I remember how as a college student
I became neurotically convinced I could hear
the audible passing of the years, continually dividing
me from myself, past from present.
Those were the days! What luxury!
Now I actually am divided, and
encounter myself in small female form,
crying. Miraculously I've exchanged
my insomnia for hers.
When we pass the clock again, I notice
it's still exactly four—hasn't budged—
but on our next swing it's somehow four-thirty.
Time cha-chas when you're having fun.
Finally I feel a change on my shoulder

as her head nods and her tension melts.
She fits so well against me
it's as though we were made together.
She's down for the night now, I know,
but just for good luck
I take an extra lap.

EEYORE'S TAIL

I am reading my son *Winnie-the-Pooh*
and recall how forty years ago my father
told me the old rope in the elm near our house
was Eeyore's tail.
When it was dry, that meant good weather.
When it was wet, then it was raining.
I think I must have made myself sick
with memory, as if not to
was to let him go, nameless as the trees.
Why else did I take so long
to marry and have children?
I still remember the slice of apple
in his tobacco pouch
and the sweet smell of his pipe smoke.
Surely it's better to forget the dead.
The small, blond head pushed against my shoulder
doesn't look like me, or him.
I read along patiently,
trying to explain the plays on words.
Then I glance at the flyleaf
and see my father's scratchy signature.
Not only is this the same story he read me
but the selfsame book, the very ink and paper.
It suddenly becomes overwhelming in my hands,
but I continue to the end, finishing
for my boy the story of how Pooh
recognized the bellpull outside Owl's house
and returned to Eeyore his lost tail.

MY NEIGHBOR'S PANTS

My ex-next-door neighbor, fired and divorced,
is staying in our TV room.
Before dinner we open a bottle of champagne
while he tells us he still can't find a job
and his daughters
are using their mother's maiden name.
That night I wake at five,
clutching my wife's knees.
I think it's because after the separation,
my father reappeared
and lived for months in the basement,
drinking and picking fights with the furnace.
The next day, to cheer him up,
we take our neighbor to the beach
where he lopes like a dog over the seaweed
and tries to talk with the gulls
in their own language.
I remember that the Bible tells us
to love our neighbors as ourselves.
But after this neighbor's finally gone,
I become convinced he switched pants on me.
The blue ones hanging in my closet
are baggy and threadbare.
An odor of failure rises from them.
I try them on,
then suddenly feel as if ants are covering me
from my ankles up to my waist.
So I rush into the backyard, rip them off,
and drown them with charcoal starter.

The gray-haired Baptist lady,
out raking her lawn,
looks at me without much surprise.
Maybe I own all the equipment of middle-class life,
but in her heart she always knew
this is what poets were like.
As the flames die down
and goosebumps swell on my legs,
all I can see left among the ashes is the label.
Only when I pick it up and read it,
do I realize I've just burned my own pants.

INTERNAL REVENUE

Trying to gauge if in the year gone by
I've profited from any "passive activity,"
scratching my noggin, feeling faintly
oxymoronic, suppressing some screams,
I suddenly realize I've incurred
a capital loss. "My head!"
I enter on Schedule D, Line 9.
"Not what it used to be. Forty-six years old.
A diminished asset." Now I've started,
what else can I write off?
Eyes, ears, hair. Pretty much expended.
Lungs, liver, knees, arches. Also
not producing their former revenue.
Surely I should be able to deduct them,
but instead of D, perhaps on Schedule A
under "Casualty and Theft Losses" since
poets have always seen time for a robber.
When I get more private, though,
my wife wryly suggests I depreciate
using the double-declining balance method.
So that would be Form 4562. Well, there.
It's nearly midnight. Entering the Post Office
with the other late citizens,
I'm weary but content, knowing
the government owes me a whopping refund.

TEE-BALL

Beyond the outfield the mimosa trees
open pink, feathery flowers in the soft air
while the boys learn to catch.
They hold their gloves horizontally
like bowls of water,
and when the ball descends, avert their faces
as if to avoid the splash. The moms,
who brought the juice and doughnut holes,
chat in their lawn chairs. A mix of men,
some in ties and Sansabelt slacks,
some with their names stitched on their shirts,
crowd the lines, yelling at their sons.
In the bottom of the fifth, the score is 45–43,
the damage controlled only by a limit
of nine batters per inning. But none
of the boys knows the score, or even
how to tally it. For the seven year olds
this afternoon is endless, the game eternal.
Only the dads care. Like swollen Thanksgiving turkeys,
they strut the sidelines, their lives accelerating
beyond repair. "Kill the ball," they yell
to the little man standing at the tee
as they glare at the American mix of dads
on the other side. And the boy swings,
lofting a high one out toward the mimosa trees.

TEETH

At the dentist, the kids' bodies, pudgy
lozenges, focus upward toward the only orifice
which tells the truth. The skeleton appears,
ring of sharp stones, Stonehenge, the ancient telescope,
the hush-hush of blood sacrifice. How can we
pretend to innocence with what our smile shows?
My liberal self-conception ended with my lips
the night of my first French kiss. The surprises
of incisors! The wet, vicious mystery of molars!
Snarling canines! The sorry sagacity of teeth
called wisdom! An expert on David Hume,
my brother-in-law at the base of his spine once grew
a marble-sized sack of "genetic debris"—tiny fingernails,
curls of hair, and teeth. A man's way of having a baby,
the remnants of a pygmy feast. Sometimes I wonder
what I've married into, but the doctors claim
it's a common occurrence. The empiricist imagines
our eyes are windows, and consciousness sits inside,
a little man, watching. At his death Hume refused
to cringe though the clerics circled his bed
waiting for the atheist to cry out. After we've become
corpses, forensics identifies us by our teeth.
The tic-tac-toe of dental work. Where does
the little man go? Hoping to avoid D.D.S. bankruptcy,
I try to teach my children how to brush. Up and down?
Back and forth? Every decade they change the philosophy.
Later when my lambs are asleep, I sneak into their room,
just for nothing slide quarters beneath their pillows.
Babies talk a lovely language of labials. Then our teeth
start with their fricatives, dentals, and snaky sibilants.
We need to listen to what they have to say.

My Garden at Night

Insomnious, I stumble
to the bathroom, kitchen, yard,
unable to let go of the dry
pumping of consciousness.
Standing in full moonlight
in yellow pajamas,
I try to remember my nightmare
about the brown water pulling me down.
The night sky is frighteningly deep.
I remember when my father,
standing by a goldfish pond,
asked whether the universe had a wall around it,
and started to laugh.
Pacing the yard, I'm surprised to find
that even at night my garden still exists.
Since I'll never get to sleep anyway,
I decide to weed
and fall on hands and knees,
pulling at the stubborn stars of crabgrass.
Gradually I forget everything
but my fingers shining in the moonlight.
I pluck at the webby roots
and breathe the dark green odor of tomato plants,
the lemon-air of marigolds.
A soft wind flows through the pine trees.
Crawling among the zucchini mounds,
I feel something dissolve
and stretch full-length in the warm dirt
under the prickly leaves and fall asleep.

MEN IN THE FLORIST'S ON VALENTINE'S DAY

Wearing our heavy winter coats,
we are lined to the counter,
each man holding a flower.
A peculiar fraternity arises among us
on this day when we are called upon
to show our hearts.
In the overheated store,
smelling of dirt and redwood bark,
a refrigeration compartment
reproduces the cold outside
and holds deck on deck of fiery roses.
The bald man in front of me
carries a pot of yellow chrysanthemums.
We are mostly middle-aged,
getting misshapen and gray,
but the day, the flowers, the buying,
even the presence of the other men,
all stir in us feelings for women.
I notice dusty tulip bulbs
packed in barrels for winter.
Outside I watch pairs of cardinals,
bright and drab, pecking in the gravel.
Beyond the parking lot,
snowdrops, little white bells,
are pushing their way above ground.

PUMPKIN LUST

Like us, the squashes in the garden, battered
by rain, have grown bulbous, warty,
speckled and rayed, mushy where they sat too long.
Surrounded by men in tall, red hats, the pope
declares married couples can commit adultery
even with each other if lust is in their hearts.
Come here, I say. O, Love, the teenage me
spent days devouring *The Ideal Marriage,*
Its Physiology and Technique with matrimony
never once in mind. What diagrams, fabulous plumbing,
faucets, union joints! Then the wild surmise, the ocean
of the little death! I shouldn't forget my fear either,
but mostly I remember the desire rolled tight in a ball.
And the sunny smell of your sheets, the Siamese kittens
playing under the bed, the hummingbirds hovering
at the ruby feeder. Since then the seasons have rained
    down,
children born, lost. So now I can no longer tell you
from the gesture you make with your hand. Our veins
have risen to the surface; our skin become smoke.
The garden lies dusted with snow, a not-so-little death.
Come, let us find a vegetable love, a pumpkin lust
which can last through years and years.

READING POETRY AT THE BIKER BAR

A snarling dog is tied near
the chopped Harleys lined like dominoes
outside the Lucky Horseshoe's door.
Entering, I think I've gone underground
it's so pitch dark,
and I slide on the sweating concrete floor
against some hairy mammoth
with a fiery Satan stitched on his jacket.
"Sorry," I say as I try
in vain to remember the karate
I took for three months at the Free School.
The bikers at the bar shout and pour beer
on each other, almost washing away the mud.
The jacket of one woman says "Mike's Property."
Another, less particular, is "Property of Road Devils."
Do they have satisfying interpersonal relationships,
    I wonder.
We poets huddle near the stage.
Maybe we have some hang-ups,
but at least we've learned to sublimate.
After Marsha recites her sestina
about migrating monarch butterflies,
the bikers stomp and shout for more
but feed the jukebox when I stand up.
Why don't we have Hemingway and Mailer with us?
Then we could bust some teeth.
But we're not even fiction writers!

Recalling my conviction
that poetry should have universal appeal,
I read my villanelle about my lost high-school love.
Suddenly the air is full of small flying objects
which ping when they hit the wall.
I turn sidewise to make a smaller target
and keep reading
as bottlecaps cover my neck and arms
with tiny serrated welts.
When we finally leave,
I feel like Orpheus emerging from Hades,
and I involuntarily turn
to see if we have left someone behind.

SOMETHING NOT THERE

On television the coyote scoots off the cliff
but hangs, his scrawny body running in place,
not knowing nothing's beneath him,
only falling after he looks down.
As my daughter lies on the couch,
I look at her inverted body
and am surprised to find her eyes
right-side up, the eyebrows underneath them,
as though she had a spiritual body
sticking out toward me.
Her face, especially the eye-crinkles,
reminds me of my father
who haunts me from beyond the grave,
his fear of female entrapment become mine,
with the help of a hundred Thurber stories,
and now weirdly realized
by his transformation into this little girl.
Last night my daughter became aware of mortality
when the grandpa died in her go-to-sleep book.
Sniffling, she wanted to know if she'd be buried
in the garden: "I thought being a person was nice."
But today she's forgotten all about it.
Even after the coyote falls miles and miles
to the canyon floor, making a small puff of dust,
he always returns in the next frame,
his flattened body springing back to shape.
What else sustains us
but the belief in something not there?

READING TO MY DAUGHTER

Thin as a bird, this child who nearly died,
she's either all-awake or all-asleep.
When I close the book, she's off in a minute.
Whereas me? I drag in-between, insomnious
at night, can't get started in the morning,
obsessed with time's erasure
until I've half-erased myself—
so when I come to read to her,
the words are marks on the page,
my mouth making the sounds, while
my brain runs on about what I should
have said to someone five hours earlier.
Scuppers the Sailor Dog banged his boat
against a rock, lived on the island for weeks,
but fixed it and started off again.
A very naughty rabbit, Peter went in
Mr. McGregor's garden, got caught in a net,
wriggled free, then returned home.
Mickey dropped into the night kitchen,
was mixed in batter, escaped, flew
his airplane, and finally fell to bed.
"Daddy," a small voice asks, "what happened
to Flora while Babar and Arthur were battling
the rhinoceroses?" Flora? Who's Flora?
The name tries to blossom in my brain
as I flip back through the pages.
This terrible war has leveled every tree;
even the birds have lost their homes.

Oh yes, Pom and Alexander's sister.
Suddenly I'm surprised to find
I'm annoyed with this innocent book.
"It doesn't say, I'm afraid." My daughter
puzzles: "Maybe she was making bandages."
Yes, that's nice. "You tell me. Wouldn't they
have to be awfully large ones?" So she
starts describing Flora's hospital
while I look in wakeful eyes
which insist, "I want to be here,
to be here, to be here."

WALLET

The cavernous supermarket gleams with light
made by excited gas dancing in tubes. Stacks
of tomatoes and cauliflowers palely yearn
after roots. Denatured music swirls people
through the store. While writing a check,
I rest my wallet on the counter,
then the brat behind me reaches out and
doesn't grab but swats it across the formica.
I wince. After years of lifting it up and down
at the two crepuscular ends of day,
I suddenly see my skinny, brown wallet
as if a surgeon plucked out a mystery organ:
"Here's your pancreas!" Four feet away, it rocks,
an emaciated leather creature, humped from
pressing against my haunch, the extra wad
of muscle propelling me through the mall.
What does it hold? My name, written nowhere else
on me, stamped on plastic cards, an accordion
playing a polka of identity. Folding money
which proclaims trust in God, exhibits it
to this extent: in exchange for hours of labor
I've accepted from my employer these pieces of paper.
And photos of my family, their enduring smiles
calling me home. Thus three appendages surely
     demonstrate
I'm not an island: my tongue, penis, and wallet—
with the last the least perishable. Salvation enough,
I suppose. So under the eyes of the brat and checkout girl,
in time to the music, I lope to recover it.

MY CAT JACK

For I will consider my Cat Jack.

For he is not like me.

For he wakes me in the morning.

For he proclaims himself with a yowl.

For when I stroke his head, he treadles my chest
   like a kitten getting milk.

For his mother is Kasha, his grandmother is Pippin,
   and his great-grandmother is Xanthippe, all living.

For he is Siamese.

For he cavorts under the sheets while I am making
   the bed.

For he stretches by kicking back his hind legs like a skier.

For he bows forward like a Mohammedan.

For he licks one paw clean, then tucks his head
   under that paw, and so the other.

For he sits on my desk and lays his ears down
   and appears to be an owl.

For he chases the balled-up poems which I discard
   on the floor and so enjoys them despite their imperfections.

For he can move each ear by itself.

For from the side I can see through his eyes like water.

For he is easy in this life.

For he does not think ahead to death.

For he carries no cash.

For he does not have any pockets.

For he saves nothing, not even a bone.

For he eats what I give him, mainly Friskies.

For he is unemployed.

For even in the cat box he maintains his dignity
  and squats very straight.
For he does not know who the president is.
For he comforts my mind, which ceaselessly rolls
  in doubt and fear.
For in the asylum Christopher Smart loved
  his Cat Jeoffrey.
For in a rational century Rousseau doted on
  feline Ninette.
For in exile Vladimir Lenin had a cat for a friend.
For in fame T. S. Eliot respected all cats.
For young Jack is a small lion in my house.
For he looks out the window for birds.
For he listens to the walls for mice.
For, despite everything,
  he is not maddened by domesticity.
For he leaps with real pleasure
  after a ribbon tied to a string.
For he inflates his tail.
For he fights with his back feet.
For in dry weather he is a bastion of electricity.
For he can find obscure heat.
For he curls about himself with his head
  upside-down.
For he sleeps.

NOTES

p. 39   *Los hombres mueren pero la patria vive para siempre:*
Men die but the nation lives forever.

p. 49   *Cochino, deme todo su dinero, pronto:*
Pig, give me all of your money, quick.

p. 51   *Allende, Allende, el pueblo te defiende:*
Allende, Allende, the people will defend you.

About the Author

Hunt Hawkins was born in Washington, D.C., in 1943. He received his B.A. from Williams College and both his M.A. and Ph.D. from Stanford University. He has received an Individual Artist Fellowship from the Florida Arts Council, a Woodrow Wilson Fellowship, and a Stanford English Department Fellowship.  His poetry has been published in *The Georgia Review, Harvard Magazine, the minnesota review, Poetry,* and *The Southern Review.* Hawkins is Professor of English at Florida State University and lives in Tallahassee, Florida, with his wife and two children.

PITT POETRY SERIES

Ed Ochester, General Editor

Archibald MacLeish, *The Great American Fourth
   of July Parade*
Peter Meinke, *Liquid Paper: New and Selected Poems*
Peter Meinke, *Night Watch on the Chesapeake*
Carol Muske, *Applause*
Carol Muske, *Wyndmere*
Leonard Nathan, *Carrying On: New & Selected Poems*
Ed Ochester and Peter Oresick, *The Pittsburgh Book of
   Contemporary American Poetry*
Sharon Olds, *Satan Says*
Alicia Suskin Ostriker, *Green Age*
Alicia Suskin Ostriker, *The Imaginary Lover*
Greg Pape, *Black Branches*
Greg Pape, *Storm Pattern*
Kathleen Peirce, *Mercy*
David Rivard, *Torque*
Liz Rosenberg, *Children of Paradise*
Liz Rosenberg, *The Fire Music*
Maxine Scates, *Toluca Street*
Richard Shelton, *Selected Poems, 1969–1981*
Betsy Sholl, *The Red Line*
Peggy Shumaker, *The Circle of Totems*
Peggy Shumaker, *Wings Moist from the Other World*
Jeffrey Skinner, *The Company of Heaven*
Leslie Ullman, *Dreams by No One's Daughter*
Constance Urdang, *Alternative Lives*
Constance Urdang, *Only the World*
Ronald Wallace, *The Makings of Happiness*
Ronald Wallace, *People and Dog in the Sun*
Belle Waring, *Refuge*
Michael S. Weaver, *My Father's Geography*
Robley Wilson, *Kingdoms of the Ordinary*
Robley Wilson, *A Pleasure Tree*
David Wojahn, *Glassworks*
David Wojahn, *Mystery Train*
Paul Zimmer, *Family Reunion: Selected and New Poems*